IF THERE IS A GOD,
WHY DO I NEED BRACES?

If There Is A God,
Why Do I Need Braces?

An Adolescent Journey to Adult Faith

JAMES PENRICE

ALBA·HOUSE   NEW·YORK

SOCIETY OF ST. PAUL, 2187 VICTORY BLVD., STATEN ISLAND, NEW YORK 10314

Library of Congress Cataloging-in-Publication Data

Penrice, James.
    If there is a God, why do I need braces: an adolescent journey
to adult faith / James Penrice.
       p.   cm.
   ISBN 0-8189-0735-5
   1. Youth — Religious life.   2. Catholic Church — Doctrines.
I. Title.
BX2355.P44   1995
248.8'3 — dc20   95-31459
                                                  CIP

Produced and designed in the United States of America by the
Fathers and Brothers of the Society of St. Paul,
2187 Victory Boulevard, Staten Island, New York 10314,
as part of their communications apostolate.

ISBN: 0-8189-0735-5

Printing Information:

Current Printing - first digit   2 3 4 5 6 7 8 9 10

Year of Current Printing - first year shown

   1999 2000 2001 2002 2003 2004 2005 2006 2007

For all the little kids I've taught
who aren't so little any more;
my love for you inspired this book.

CONTENTS

Don't let the excitement of your youth
cause you to forget about your Creator.
Honor him in your youth.

Ecclesiastes 12:1

Some of these people have missed
the most important thing in life —
They don't know God.

1 Timothy 6:21

IF THERE IS A GOD,
WHY DO I NEED BRACES?

Part One:
THE TRUTH ABOUT GOD

They say there's a heaven for those
    who will wait,
Some say it's better, but I say it ain't.
I'd rather laugh with the sinners than
    cry with the saints;
The sinners are much more fun.
You know that only the good die young.
Billy Joel

You'll never get to heaven by being good. It's a place for sinners only.

That may be the last thing you'd expect to read in a book about God, but it's true — the Bible says so. You'll *never* get to heaven by *being good*. It's a place for *sinners only* — the Bible says so! If this sounds shocking, it's only because you haven't yet learned who God *really* is and how he *really* works in your life. Up until now you've learned the "little kid" version of God, the one who comes with easy answers, strict rules and stern expectations. But you're only now becoming old enough to really understand some of the more complicated aspects of God which you weren't able to learn as a child.

When we're little we learn about God in very simple terms because he's really very hard to understand; we can't see him with our eyes or hear him with our ears. Adults give us very easy answers to our questions about God because to *really* know him takes maturity we simply don't have yet. It's not that they don't want us to learn — they just don't want to confuse us with a lot of ideas we're not yet ready to understand. So they usually teach religion in terms of rules, rewards and punishments.

But as we get older, our lives become more complicated and our minds become more mature. We begin to question everything we've been taught, especially *why* these rules exist. The easy answers of childhood no longer make any sense. As a result, everything we learn as children needs to be "upgraded" as we get older, to meet the growing needs of our more complicated lives.

Unfortunately, some people never go beyond their childhood ideas about God. They never lose the image of a bearded old man watching from the sky with a scorecard, keeping track of our every move so he can "zap" us when we do wrong and reward us when we do good. They grow up never learning who God really is. As a result they often end up rebelling against him, as Billy Joel's song indicates. I think that's a terrible shame, because I believe with all my heart that God is the answer to *all* the questions and problems of our lives. He's not a stern old man looking to take away people's joy or to punish them for every mistake. He welcomes *all* people, *especially* sinners, and offers them a love so strong it's hard to understand by our human standards. We all need lots of love in our lives, to have someone who will always accept us, encourage us and never give up on us no matter how bad we may be or how many mistakes we might make. For me and for millions of others, God is that kind of a friend. I'd like him to be yours too.

I'm writing this book to help you learn more about God as you leave your childhood and begin to grow into a young adult. I hope this book will help you "upgrade" your information about God, so that you may begin to grow into a *mature* relationship with him which will take you far beyond your childhood notions. This is a time of your life when you're going to need a strong, supportive friend, because a lot of changes will be happening to you. In the midst of these changes you'll need something strong to hang onto for strength and support. I want to help you form a relationship with God that will bring you more love, more joy, more peace, more acceptance and more fulfillment than you'll ever find in anything else. But the things you learned about God as a child won't help you anymore as you begin to seriously question his role in your life. I know — I've been on that journey myself.

When I was a kid, everything I had ever learned about God and religion could be summed up in two simple little words: "Be good." That seemed to be the point of it all. God wanted me to "be good." Jesus wanted me to "be good." Any kind of success in life (and any chance of getting to go to heaven) seemed to revolve around my ability to "be good." So as long as I obeyed my parents, cleaned my room, got along with my brothers and sister, did my homework, brushed my teeth, combed my hair and blew my nose, God would be happy and everything would be okay.

But since "being bad" was so much easier (and a heck of a lot more fun!) I learned that there was a "system" in place to keep me in line to "be good." I learned that God is "up" in heaven and we're "down" on earth, and that God watches us closely as we live our lives. He gives us the ten commandments as rules to follow, Jesus as an example of how to live, and the Holy Spirit as a guide to teach us. But then it's up to us to "be good." God supposedly keeps track of how many times we're "good" and how many times we're "bad," and rewards and punishes us accordingly. When we die God compares how many times we've been "good" to how many times we've been "bad," and depending on whichever is greater, sends us either to heaven or to hell forever.

This whole plan made sense to me then, because that's the way the rest of the world worked. My parents and teachers made rules, then it was up to me to follow them. If I obeyed I was rewarded; if I disobeyed I was punished. That's how everything else in the world worked, so why wouldn't God work in the same way?

But as I grew older I began to wonder about this scheme, and about my place in it. I had been taught that I could only get to heaven by "being good." But I had done a lot of "bad" things in my life, and I knew by my nature that I would continue to do "bad" things. I had times where I went through sadness and confusion, and I thought that was God's way of punishing me for being "bad." I went through times when it felt like God had left my life, given up on me, because I just wasn't "good" enough to be counted among his children.

There was never a time when I stopped believing in God. But there was a time when I didn't like him very much. When I tried to be "good" like he wanted I would sometimes be laughed at and picked on, and I couldn't see much reward in that. When I was sinful and bad things were happening to me I felt worthless, that God had become disappointed in me, and I became angry with him. God was supposed to love me; but I was, after all, only human. I was bound to do "bad" things, to make mistakes, to sin. Why would God punish me simply for being human, especially when he was the one who made me human? Why would he want me to always "be good" when it was impossible to always "be good," and he knew it? I felt like rebelling against God and his whole plan of "being good." God was making unrealistic demands of me, and I just couldn't see the sense of following him anymore.

The things I had been taught about God as a child were now useless to me. They no longer provided the answers to the very serious questions I had about God and about my life. I needed to find something more, something that spoke to me as an adult and would make more sense in my more complicated world.

To look for answers, I began for the first time to *carefully* read the Bible. I had always been told that this book (which up to then I had always thought was pretty boring) had all the answers, so I thought I'd better start finding some. I began reading the letters of St. Paul, which were written to teach people about God in the very early days of the Christian church. While reading the first of his letters, the one to the Romans, I came across a passage that turned my life around. It shattered all my childhood ideas about "being good" and God's rewards and punishments, and spoke more *realistically* about what life was actually like. It didn't talk about "goody-goody" rules or pie-in-the-sky ideas. It described the way *I* felt, described my struggles with sin and self-worth — and it was written by a *saint*! This passage helped me begin to empty myself of guilt and my sense of worthlessness — my sense of being "bad" — so I could be filled with the *truth* about God's love for me and how it really works. The passage went like this:

> I don't understand myself at all, for I really want to do what is right, but I can't. I do what I don't want to — what I hate. I know perfectly well that what I am doing is wrong, and my bad conscience proves that I agree with these laws I am breaking. But I can't help myself. . . . No matter which way I turn I can't make myself do right. I want to but I can't. When I want to do good, I don't; and when I try not to do wrong, I do it anyway. Now if I am doing what I don't want to, it is plain where the trouble is: sin still has me in its evil grasp.   *Romans 7:15-20*

I couldn't believe my eyes. I thought the Bible was written by holy people who were supposed to tell us how to "be good." But here was St. Paul, the author of about a third of the New Testament and one of the greatest saints in the history of the church, saying that it's *impossible* to "be good," that even he is forever caught up in sin. The Bible actually says that this "be good" thing is not something we can do on our own. I was starting to have respect for God again, and became eager to learn more about how he *really* works.

But there were still more answers to find. Obviously God *wants* his people to "be good," but if the Bible says that we can't, and they're *both* right, how can this possibly make sense? How do obvious sinners like Paul get to heaven and become saints if the only way to get there is to "be good"? It must be that "being good" is *not* the way to find God's love and to get to heaven. As it turns out, it's not!

The answer came in another section of the letter to the Romans, one that explains in a nutshell what Christianity is *really* all about. Read it very carefully:

> But now God has shown us a different way to heaven — not by "being good enough" and trying to keep his laws, but by a new way (though not new,

really, for the Scriptures told about it long ago). Now God says he will accept and acquit us — declare us "not guilty" — if we trust Jesus Christ to take away our sins. And we all can be saved in this same way, by coming to Christ, no matter who we are or what we have been like. Yes, all have sinned; all fall short of God's glorious ideal; yet now God declares us "not guilty" of offending him if we trust in Jesus Christ, who in his kindness freely takes away our sins. For God sent Christ Jesus to take the punishment for our sins and to end all God's anger against us. He used Christ's blood and our faith as the means of saving us from his wrath.

Romans 3:21-25

Paul teaches the same idea later in Romans:

But didn't he earn his right to heaven by all the good things he did? No, for being saved is a gift; if a person could earn it by being good, then it wouldn't be free — but it is! It is given to those who do not work for it. For God declares sinners to be good in his sight if they have faith in Christ to save them from God's wrath. *Romans 4:4-5*

And again:

> We aren't saved from sin's grasp by knowing the commandments of God because we can't and don't keep them, but God put into effect a different plan to save us. He sent his own Son in a human body like ours — except that ours are sinful — and destroyed sin's control over us by giving himself as a sacrifice for our sins.   *Romans 8:3*

And in Galatians:

> How different from this way of faith is the way of law, which says that a man is saved by obeying every law of God, without one slip. But Christ has bought us out from under the doom of that impossible system by taking the curse for our wrongdoing upon himself.
> *Galatians 3:12-13*

And in Ephesians:

> Salvation is not a reward for the good we have done, so none of us can take any credit for it.   *Ephesians 2:9*

And again in Romans:

> So it is that we are saved by faith in
> Christ and not by the good things we
> do.   *Romans 3:28*

Get the point?

These passages really helped me make sense
of things, and I began to find answers that had
never occurred to me before. I learned that religion
is not about rules, rewards and punishments. It's
about *love*, and the powerful change that takes
place in us when we choose to accept God and the
incredible love he has for us. It's about the change
that takes place in us when we let go of our feelings
of worthlessness, shame, sinfulness and guilt and
allow ourselves to be loved with a love so strong it
created the world and everything in it. No conditions, no scorecards, no punishments. Just love —
and lots of it.

No matter who we are, what we believe, what
we want out of life, or how we act, all of us need to
be loved. We need to feel that we're worthwhile,
that our life makes a difference. Love changes us so
we can feel that. It makes us feel good about
ourselves, turns us away from selfishness and
sadness, makes us want to do good things for
ourselves and for others. Love makes us happy.

When we feel loved by someone totally,
completely, without rules, conditions, rewards or
punishments, and when we know that love lasts

forever whether we deserve it or not — we change. We become more loving of ourselves and of others, wanting to return that love in a spirit of joy and thankfulness. That's when we no longer need rules — the love we've accepted into our hearts makes us *want* to do "good." In fact, to be loved so strongly and so completely means we *are* good. Period. No scorecards, no punishments, just love.

That's what religion is all about — simply accepting the incredible love of God and letting it change our lives for the better. My mistake was in thinking that God was "out there" somewhere, merely watching us, giving us the rules to follow and then sitting back to see how we do. But God loves us too much to just sit back and watch. He wants to be a *part* of our lives and *help* lead us to the goodness that will bring us real happiness. It is not up to us at all to "be good" — it is up to us to give ourselves to God so that *his* goodness can work *through* us and make us "good," bringing us more joy and peace than we could possibly get by ourselves. And he's willing to put up with a lot of mistakes — more than you might think — in order to bring us to his goodness.

That's why I began this book with those outrageous but true statements: "You'll never get to heaven by being good. It's a place for sinners only." Being good isn't the way to heaven, because we just can't do it all the time. We get to heaven by *believing in Jesus Christ*, trying our best to follow him, and trusting that *he* has already taken the punishment for the sins we do commit. Thus only sinners get to heaven, because *everyone* is a sinner. Heaven is full of *forgiven* sinners, whom God has welcomed home with his forgiveness simply because they asked for it and trusted in Jesus to get it.

It sure beats the image of the old man in the sky waiting to zap us!

When you take a close look at what the Bible really teaches us about God, it's hard to understand how anybody would not be attracted to this tremendous love or would not want it as a part of their life. Jesus tells a story about a rebellious son who runs away from home and spends his father's money living wildly. When he returns home he receives his father's forgiveness simply by asking for it. Jesus says this is the kind of love that God has for us. He doesn't criticize sinners and put them down — he *looks* for them to come to him and welcomes them with open arms. How could anyone not be attracted to that kind of God? And how could anyone not want to return that kind of love by living for him?

My adult view of God is very different from that of my childhood, and much more meaningful. Stated simply, it goes like this:

The one God has existed from all eternity in three Persons: the Father, the Son, and the Holy Spirit.

God created the world and all its people out of pure love. He created people so he could share his love and the beauties of his work with them. God also gave people the freedom to either accept him or reject him — letting them fully know the consequences of either choice. The consequence of accepting him is to experience his love and the happiness it brings; not accepting him means living apart from his love and the sadness that brings. He did this because pure love means giving people the freedom to make their own choices — not forcing something upon them but inviting someone to love.

If people chose to live for God, he realized they were bound to sin and to make mistakes. They would need to be punished for breaking their promise to live for him, but he loves people too much to give them the punishment they truly deserve. So the Father sent Jesus as his Son in human form to take the punishment for everyone's sins by his crucifixion. He also gave the promise that anyone who truly believes in his Son and does their best to follow him will have their sins forgiven and will join him in heaven. After Jesus' resurrection, the third divine Person, the Holy Spirit, was sent to enlighten Jesus' followers and give life to the church. It is in Jesus that all our imperfections are made up for, so that we can one day reach perfection with God. That's what it means when we say that Jesus takes away our sins — we still sin, but Jesus takes away the punishment which is truly due to us for sinning so that we can be united with God forever.

There is nothing in the world that can compare to a genuine, mature relationship with God. As young people begin to grow up they're faced with many problems, and they need lots of love, comfort and acceptance. There are many different things young people look to for this comfort, none of which comes close to the fulfillment found in knowing God.

Some look to smoking. Ever since we were babies, there's always been a natural instinct to suck on something for comfort. We receive our first nourishment by sucking on milk. We're given pacifiers to soothe us when we're upset. So it's only natural that as adults we sometimes turn to that basic instinct to comfort us in times of stress.

While smoking can give us comfort, it also has some very dangerous side-effects. It causes disease which destroys the bodies God created and can lead to a much earlier death. It also makes us less attractive by yellowing our teeth and fingers, ruining our breath and dirtying other people's air. The comfort smoking gives is only temporary — its ultimate end is discomfort, illness and death. We need a source of comfort that is much more healthy and lasting.

Some look to alcohol and to drugs. These are chemicals we put inside our bodies to change the way we feel when we don't like what we're feeling. Sometimes we use them merely out of curiosity, to find out what they'll do to us. Many times we use them just to belong to a group, since so many other people use them. Alcohol and drugs can give us a sense of security, comfort and belonging, which is why so many people look to them.

Yet like smoking, drugs and alcohol provide only temporary comfort — our problems are still there when we sober up — along with the additional problems of sickness and possibly becoming addicted. They also have very dangerous side-effects. They make us lose control of our actions, putting us in danger of hurting ourselves and other people. The chemicals themselves can poison and seriously damage our bodies, possibly leading to early death. We often think we're finding acceptance from others and self-worth by using drugs and alcohol. But if people only accept us if we use them, *we're* not really being accepted at all. It is the chemical that is being accepted, and a relationship based on that is very weak. Real love and friendship have nothing to do with whether or not a person smokes, drinks or uses drugs. They're based on acceptance of people as they *are*. Period.

You can't rely on a chemical for self-esteem or acceptance, because by doing so you're saying that the chemical is more important than *you*. Naturally this will only make you feel worse about yourself. It takes strength to *be yourself* without having to rely on an outside substance for your self-worth. That kind of strength can't be found in any drink or drug. We have to look to something much more powerful.

Some look to sex. Sex is not only a lot of fun, it makes us feel tremendously loved. To wrap our body around another person and have them hold us, kiss us and give us pleasure seems the perfect answer to loneliness and worthlessness. It makes us feel cared for. Yet while sex *is* the greatest gift of love one person can give to another, when it is not used in the right circumstances it can be devastating.

Casual sex can make us even lonelier than the loneliness which led us to it. Sex makes us as close to another person as is humanly possible; but if our relationship with that person later ends, it causes great emotional pain. Nothing hurts more inside than being loved deeply by someone and then having that love come to an end. Too many young people become involved in sex with partners who later leave their lives. The pain and emptiness this causes later hurts their ability to love and trust others in more lasting relationships. The only time sex really works as a way to find comfort and love is when it is with someone with whom you have made a *lifelong commitment*, or *promise*, to love — where the love is shared in order to *strengthen the family bond and commitment* between you — not just to have fun or to use that person for enjoyment. Having sex just for fun without a genuine love for the other person can not only lead to hurt, it makes us more self-centered and less caring, which eventually leads to more loneliness and sadness in the future.

These are some of the riskier answers many young people find to coping with the problems in their lives. There are, of course, many more positive ways to find happiness: friends, music, sports, hobbies, etc. But all of these answers, as good as they are, still are only temporary solutions. Like all things of this world, they won't last forever.

The only way to find the kind of love, comfort and acceptance that will last forever is to look to the only thing that *does* last forever — God. It's really quite simple. Since God is the creator of the world, the only way to find happiness in it is to follow his ways. Following anyone else's ways besides our creator's simply won't work. If you bought a new computer, you wouldn't read the owner's manual from your parents' car to learn how to run it. Since the car company didn't design the computer, their guidelines would be useless. Only the computer's maker can give you the right instructions to follow to make sure your computer works well. You can follow your own ideas, and they may work for awhile, but they won't work nearly as well as the designer's. You'll eventually run into problems which only the computer's designer can solve for you.

In the same way, the world can only work well when it follows its designer's instructions. Following any other way may seem to work for awhile, but it only leads to more problems. It's really just common sense — for the world to run smoothly, we must follow the ways of the one who created it. Only he has the real answers, and he's the only way to find real goodness and truth.

So how do you get to know this God, how do you make him a *real, meaningful* part of your life, not just some idea that's been passed on to you? That's what we'll be looking at in this book. Come along with me, and I'll tell you more about him.

God is very mysterious and very difficult to completely understand. I can't give you the answers to all your questions about him, and I can't explain him in full. I can't give you a relationship with God, because that in itself is a gift only God can give to those who truly seek him.

But I can give you enough information to get you started on your search for a mature, adult relationship with God. When you're through with this book you'll have many answers, but you'll still have many questions. Learning about God is really a life-long process. But I hope that the answers you find in these pages will help direct you in that *life-long search* for answers. It will be a wonderful and meaningful search if you trust, believe and follow.

So let's begin. In Part Two we will see if we can "upgrade" your information about God by answering some of the most commonly asked questions about him.

I sincerely hope that your reading of this book will bring you much closer to God and to the beautiful things his love has in store for you. I also hope it will make you feel great about yourself as one of his beautiful creations. May he bless you with every good thing as you begin your journey. St. Paul can show you how to start:

> It's like this: when I was a child I spoke and thought and reasoned as a child does. But when I became a man my thoughts grew far beyond those of my childhood, and now I have put away the childish things. In the same way, we can see and understand only a little about God now, as if we were peering at

his reflection in a poor mirror; but someday we are going to see him in his completeness, face to face. Now all that I know is hazy and blurred, but then I will see everything clearly, just as clearly as God sees into my heart right now.

1 Corinthians 13:11-12

Part Two:
QUESTIONS AND ANSWERS

Is there really a God?

This is the best place to begin, because if we're going to spend our lives dedicated to some mysterious being we should have some assurance that he's actually there.

To be honest, there is no way of knowing for sure if God really exists. Our belief in God is exactly that — *a belief*. Faith means believing in something that can't be proven by our senses. But in order to believe in something that we can't prove, we need pretty convincing evidence for it. We've got plenty of evidence to suggest that God exists, and that's where we start in building our relationship with him. I'd like to tell you some of the reasons *why I* believe in the existence of God.

When I look at everything that exists in the world, and the remarkable order and precision with which they run — the complexity of the human body, the varieties of animal and plant life, the water cycle and food chains which keep them all alive, the beauty and power of an ocean, the majesty of a mountain, the immensity of a starry sky — I find it very difficult to believe that all of these remarkable creations came to be simply by chance or by accident. No random chemical reaction could form the abundance and diversity of life or design each one so carefully that even the most minor details — from breathing to photosynthesis, from evaporation to reproduction — could be so precisely planned and carried out. There has to be some being of remarkable intelligence for our world to be created with such complicated yet well-working designs.

The human body is a perfect example. It is simply too intricate not to have been designed by some superior being. Your body has a complex system of cells, tissues and organs that interact with each other automatically without your having to consciously control them. You don't have to make your heart beat or your lungs breathe — they're *designed* to work independently. Your digestive system processes the nutrients from your food and gets rid of the waste automatically. When you get a cut or a broken bone your body miraculously heals itself. The human body is truly a remarkable machine which even the most intelligent person in the history of the world couldn't figure out how to build.

As human beings we like to think we're pretty smart and independent. We're able to build some pretty amazing things. But none of us made our own bodies, nor could we. Our parents didn't even make us. They performed the act through which the egg in your mother's womb was fertilized, but your mother didn't make the egg and your father didn't make the sperm. Someone had to design this process and put the parts there to start with.

During the nine months you were in your mother's womb, your mother really had nothing to do with the process of actually building you. She didn't get up in the morning and say, "Let's see, today I'll make the hands, and tomorrow I'll work on the feet. Next week I'll get the nervous system in place, then I'll work on the circulatory system. I'd better get that digestive tract in place before we go on vacation. The eyes and ears will have to wait until we get home." Nope. Your mother simply waited for you lovingly while you were formed inside of her by some unseen, powerfully creative force.

Take the same kind of look at *all* of the life which exists in nature, and you'll see the same level of advanced design. Much too intelligent for the human mind to create, and much too advanced to be caused by some mere chemical reaction.

One of the criticisms many non-believers have is that religious people don't "think for themselves." I once saw a sign that said, "Reason, not religion." My answer to that is simple. It's true we have to think for ourselves about many things. But as soon as I meet someone who can reason well enough to design and build a butterfly, a dolphin, a redwood tree or a human being, then I'll look to "reason" over religion. But as long as there appears to be a being of supreme intelligence who created the world and all that is in it, I'll trust in that being to do the major "reasoning," and I'll follow trustingly in his ways.

That is why I believe there is a God who *created* the world. But why do I believe that God not only *made* the world but *exists* and *acts* in it, *participating* in the lives of people? To answer this, let's again examine the human body, but this time from an *emotional* point of view rather than the physical.

It's obvious that we're much more than a biological system, however advanced it may be. We do more than eat, sleep, go to the bathroom and reproduce ourselves. We have a mysterious emotional side which can't be easily explained by science. We love, laugh, cry, imagine, remember. We feel joy, sadness, anger, jealousy, loneliness, hurt. While we feel these things inside our bodies we have no biological explanation for them. Often they seem to come from nowhere.

For example, a scientist can tell us how tears are manufactured in the tear ducts, and how they travel to the eyes. But when asked how the experience of being called a bad name triggers this response, it would be impossible to explain from a biological point of view. A scientist can explain what muscles move when we smile, but can't give us a physical cause for why seeing a loved one enter the room causes us to do this. All the scientific research we could do could never explain the root causes of our emotional responses.

The point is this — our bodies are much more than instruments for biological processes — they are also the place where complex emotional actions take place. We have nothing to firmly attribute these to, but we know they're *real* — they exist though we can't explain them. Emotions are also the *only* things which have been common to *all* human beings in *all* ages of history. The human body has changed considerably through the years — on the average people have gotten taller through the ages, have gotten healthier, have lived longer. Yet emotions have remained constant throughout history. People have *always* experienced the same *feelings*, no matter how much the body has changed.

From this I conclude that the body, as wonderful as it is, is only temporary, but emotions are forever. There is a mysterious, spiritual reality which has been part of humankind since the beginning of time, even though the body has gone through many structural changes. There is an eternal spirit in whose image we are made. This eternal spirit is God. He is the ultimate reason for our living, and deserves our devotion as the center, beginning and end of our existence.

If God created the world and all of its wonders, just think how important we are that he included us in his creation! A priest I once knew described it very movingly. He said that by creating us, God said, "Even with my stars and planets, mountains and rivers, rainbows and flowers, valleys and plains, and all the other wonders of creation — my world just wouldn't be complete without *you* in it!" That's how important we all are — the creator of the universe personally chose us to be in it!

I once wrote a prayer while thinking about how awesome it is not only to be made by the same being who created all of the world's wonders, but to also have the honor of being a friend of his. It went like this:

Father. What better name to call you, my creator, my all-loving God who formed me in your hands and who continues to form me. What a joy it is to spend time with the creator of the universe, and what an awesome privilege. To think that the one who created the earth, the sun, the moon, the stars, the oceans and rivers, mountains, grasses, all the animals of the earth and all life everywhere, searches for *me*, for a personal relationship with *me*! What an awesome joy to be loved by so powerful a being, and to be made by his loving hands.

Lord, you created the universe. With just a fraction of your power in me, imagine what I could do! Help me to find that power, to create for you your Kingdom on earth, to love it with your abundant love, and create it as beautifully as you. Help me to strive each day to live not for myself but for you, to bring your loving kindness to all that I meet.

Father, sometimes I find it hard to believe that you could still love me despite some of the things I do. When I think of how you love me totally no matter how often I fail, it fills me with a strength and desire to make myself truly worthy of that love. Sometimes I ask, "What did I ever do to deserve the love of the creator of the world?" Then I realize I didn't have to do anything. It was given to me for *free*! It was paid for by your Son, who willingly gave all out of, again, that total, unconditional love he has for me. When I feel the strength in that same love I want to do nothing else but to share it with others. Help me to know the depth of your love, so that I can bring it to others in the spirit of your joy.

Thank you for my life and for your many blessings in it. Thank you for loving me, even though I often don't deserve it.

When you in your infinite genius, O God, created the earth, the sun, the moon, the stars, the seas, the mountains, the rivers, valleys, birds, animals, rainbows, winds, clouds, flowers and trees — thanks for also thinking of me!

What about Jesus? How does he fit into all of this?

Very few people will argue that Jesus actually existed as a person. Even people who don't believe in God recognize Jesus at least as an historical figure who really lived on the earth. But Jesus claimed to be the Son of God, God himself in human form. He said he was sent into the world not only to teach us how God wants us to live but to lead us to God. Jesus died on the cross then rose to new life for one reason: so that *anyone* who believes in him and follows him as the Son of God will be *joined* to his death and thus also be raised to new life. His death and resurrection are *our* promise of death to this temporary world and never-ending life in the next.

Sounds pretty good — but can we believe it? Again, Jesus' claim to be God made flesh can't be positively proven, but there's enough evidence to lead us to accept it in faith. I'd like to tell you some of the reasons *why I* believe Jesus is the Son of God and our Savior.

One reason is the report of so many people throughout history, and what people had to go through to defend their faith. The most important testimony comes from the people who worked the most closely with Jesus on earth — the apostles.

When the news got around that Jesus had risen from the dead, many people thought it was a hoax. They thought someone had stolen Jesus' body and hidden it, so his followers could make the claim that he had risen from the dead.

But judging from the actions of Jesus' closest friends after the resurrection, it is highly unlikely that it was a hoax.

The apostles spent the rest of their lives travelling to far away countries spreading the good news about Jesus and how people can go to God through him. They were laughed at, arrested, persecuted and tortured, and all but one of them were killed for teaching about Jesus by people who were afraid that Christianity was a threat to their power over people. To risk the danger and humiliation they had to endure, and to choose to be *killed* rather than to renounce Jesus as the Son of God — the apostles had to be fully convinced that this man they knew was for real and that the message of Jesus was true. And if these were the people who knew him *personally* on earth, then I believe their teaching. These men were with Jesus before the crucifixion and saw him after the resurrection. None of them would go through torture and death for teaching about Jesus if they thought there was even the possibility of a hoax. They were convinced he was actually God's Son, and that convinces me.

In the centuries since, thousands upon thousands have endured the same hardships in order to bring the news of Jesus to others. Missionaries have given their lives to bring the gospel into hostile countries where Jesus' name was not yet known.

Some 2,000 years later, the message of Jesus is as alive as it was when he walked the earth. No other figure in history has been as important to so many people through so many centuries as has this man from Nazareth. His influence is so powerful that it can't be merely his *memory* causing so much action — he has to be *actually present* himself. Only the Son of God could have such a strong spiritual presence through so much time and throughout so many places in the world.

Jesus also shows so much wisdom in his

teachings, wisdom far beyond the knowledge of mere human beings, that I believe it can only come from God. Furthermore, Jesus has a tremendous capacity to love even the most evil person, a characteristic we usually associate only with God. When I think of the love Jesus showed for the people who crucified him, I'm awestruck — this is the unexplainable, unbelievable love of God showing through a human being who must be God himself to have that profound a love.

Think about it: Jesus was falsely convicted and sentenced to death. He was tied to a post and whipped until his back was torn and bloodied. A crown of sharp thorns was painfully shoved onto his head and a heavy wooden cross was dumped on his back. He had to carry that cross while mobs of people (the people he was doing this for!) laughed at him, spit at him, threw garbage at him and called him names. His hands and feet were brutally nailed to that cross and it was stuck in the ground so he could die in the most undignified manner possible.

Jesus had every reason to hate these people, but he realized that people who are the meanest are the ones who need love the most. They needed Jesus to go through this torture so that *they* could come back to God. He prayed that God would forgive them for these terrible things they had done to him.

The human reaction would be to hate these

people or to wish them evil, but God's love endures the most bitter insults and agonizing pain, and remains committed to people and loving them no matter what they do.

Those are just a few of the reasons I believe in Jesus as the Son of God. I also believe because of the friendship I have formed with him over the years. We'll talk more about getting to know God and Jesus later in the book.

Who is the Holy Spirit?

Let us begin by saying that we are dealing here with a mystery, namely, the fact that there is one God in three divine Persons —Father, Son and Holy Spirit. Each of the Persons has a relationship to the other two and with each one of us. I am going to try to explain this in words which I hope will help you to understand the mystery better, though admittedly in an imperfect way.

God is our Father, the creator of the entire universe. God is our Savior, Jesus, who became human to live our life, die our death, and rise from the dead so that we might share his never-ending life. God is also the Holy Spirit, the one who makes us holy. When Jesus returned to heaven and was no longer *physically* here on the earth, God the Holy Spirit came so he could always be present in the world. The Holy Spirit is the driving force through which God works in our lives. We are given the Holy Spirit first in baptism, then more fully in confirmation. It is the source from which we get the strength to live our lives according to God's designs.

It is impossible for us to understand how there are three different Persons at once — Father, Son and Holy Spirit — in the one God. God is not one Person but three distinct Persons. The Father relates to the Son and to the Holy Spirit; the Son relates to the Father and to the Holy Spirit; and the Holy Spirit relates to the Father and to the Son. Each of these Persons is a separate "identity" in God. As Father, God is the creator-designer whose instructions need to be followed for the world to work properly. As the Son, he became incarnate as Jesus, who died and rose again so that we will be able to live with God forever. As the Holy Spirit, he lives within us and helps us experience our relationship with the Triune God. Each person of the Trinity plays an important role in our lives, and makes God available to us.

If God loves us, why do so many bad things happen to us?

This is a question asked by many people struggling with the question of whether or not God really exists. How can a God with the power to do anything allow suffering in the lives of the people he loves? Why doesn't he stop wars, hunger, poverty, crime, disease, death, accidents, natural disasters? If God really exists he would hate to see his people suffer, to see his creation being destroyed. Why doesn't he do something about it?

To answer this question, we first have to understand what love really is, because the world has some very different notions about love which simply don't match God's ideas. Let's begin by first defining what real love is, then we'll answer this question more specifically.

First of all, love is not a *feeling*. Many people think that when they have a feeling of affection for another person that this is love. But our feelings are never stable — they come and go with our different moods. Sometimes we feel so "in love" with a person, yet at other times we become angry with them and feel like we don't even like them. Our feelings are fickle and very misleading. Love can't be based on feelings, because feelings are always changing. That kind of love will never last.

Love is rather a *commitment*, or *promise*, we make to always care for another person — even during the times we *don't feel like it*! Many times relationships end because people say they "don't love" someone anymore. What they're really saying is that the romantic *feeling* they had toward that person has ended. Real love never ends — it perseveres despite the ups and downs of feelings, committing itself to helping someone no matter what you may be feeling at a given moment. In fact, real love perseveres in the *toughest* times, never giving up on someone no matter how hopeless the circumstances might seem.

The next thing we have to understand about love is more specific to our question. Love does not try to *control* people or the events in their lives. Loving someone means respecting their *freedom* to be themselves and to make their own choices. We have to love people the way they *are*, not the way we *want them to be*. Forcing someone to do things against their will to please our wishes is not love at all — we're loving our *idea* of how we'd like them to be, not who they really *are*.

There is a famous saying which has been printed many times on posters, greeting cards and other memorabilia, and it goes something like this: If you love someone, let them go free. If they don't return, they were never meant for you in the first place. If they return, hold them close to your heart forever.

That's the kind of love God has for us. He respects our freedom to make choices, he doesn't force himself on anyone. He loves us so much that he made us completely free, and that means free to reject him. He doesn't seek to control us. Sure, God is all powerful and loves us more than we could ever imagine. But he can't control our lives for us because he didn't make us to become his "puppets." He made us to be free to make our own decisions, and being free means accepting the consequences for our own poor decisions.

But because God loves us, he'll be there to comfort us when the world causes us pain. That's where God's love and compassion come in — not in stopping suffering, but being there to heal the wounds, offer help to overcome our hardships. God came into the world not to stop suffering, but to fill the suffering world with his comforting presence.

When you love someone you hurt when they're hurting, and you try to help ease the pain. You can't always stop bad things from happening, but you can be there to *comfort* them once bad things happen. You can warn someone about the potential danger of their actions, but love means giving people the freedom to make their own mistakes, to learn from them, and to always be there to comfort them when they are hurt. That's exactly how God's love works in our lives. He warns us about potential dangers and tells us what he'd *like* us to do, but then lets us make our decisions. We then have to live with the consequences, good or bad.

Suffering in the world is not caused by God — it is caused by our human imperfection. Humans are imperfect because they have not strived for the perfection God offers in accepting his love and his kind of life. Wars and crime are caused by people's anger, not God's. Poverty and hunger are the result of people's greed and unwillingness to share their wealth, not by any fault of God's. Disease and death occur because our bodies are only temporary, and therefore imperfect. Natural disasters occur because the earth is also a temporary, imperfect home.

While God's love does not control human actions and therefore allows suffering, his love does make him present to comfort and strengthen people when they are in trouble. His comfort comes from our neighbors who have accepted God into their lives and have made a commitment to share his love with others. It is through the love of family and friends in times of trouble that we experience God despite suffering.

A story I once heard on a retreat may help to illustrate this point.

One day a man was relaxing in the rocking chair on his front porch when a friend drove up in a pick-up truck. "The dam just broke," his friend shouted. "The whole town will be flooded in minutes. Get in the truck and I'll drive you to safety."

"No thanks," the man answered. "God will save me. You go on your way."

His friend shrugged his shoulders in puzzlement and drove off.

The flood waters came crashing down the street, and soon the man's house was half-covered in water. As he sat on the roof of his porch watching it all, another friend came by in a boat.

"There's more water on the way," his friend said. "Get in my boat and I'll take you to safety."

"That's okay," replied the man. "God will save me. You go on your way."

Puzzled, his friend drove off in the boat.

Soon the entire house was covered with water, and the man sat on the top of his chimney.

A helicopter hovered overhead, and an emergency worker spoke to him through a loudspeaker.

"We'll lower the rope ladder. Climb up and we'll rescue you."

"Don't bother," said the man. "God will save me. You go on your way."

So the helicopter left. Shortly afterwards, the man drowned.

When he got to heaven the man stormed up to God in a fit of anger.

"I'm so angry with you!" the man screamed. "All my life I believed in you, I trusted in you to take care of me. But in my hour of most dire need you did absolutely nothing to help me!"

"What do you mean I didn't do anything?" replied God. "I sent you a truck, a boat and a helicopter!"

Yes, bad things do happen, but God will always be there to help us through bad times. We just have to learn how and where to look for him. And we have to remember the real meaning of love:

> Love is very patient and kind, never jealous or envious, never boastful or proud, never haughty or selfish or rude. Love does not demand its own way. It is not irritable or touchy. It does not hold grudges and will hardly even notice when others do it wrong. It is never glad about injustice, but rejoices whenever truth wins out. If you love someone, you will be loyal to him no matter what the cost. You will always believe in him, always expect the best of him, and always stand your ground in defending him.   *1 Corinthians 13:4-7*

How can God be involved in the lives of so many different people at the same time?

I've wondered about this question for a long time. I know God is great and all-powerful, but there are *millions* of people who look to him and pray to him every day. How can he possibly listen to all these people, keep track of them all, and be active in each of their lives?

While I can't explain *exactly* how God works, I can give you a pretty good example that may help you understand how it is possible for a great and mighty being to be in so many places at the same time. It occurred to me one day while I was vacationing in Florida, and demonstrates how God teaches us through the symbols of his creation, if we pay attention to them and listen for his wisdom.

I was walking along the beach at the Gulf of Mexico. The sand was very hot, and there were a lot of hidden thorns sticking their sharp points into my feet. Between the heat and the thorns my feet were taking quite a pounding, and needed to be soothed if I was going to continue on my journey. Luckily, comfort wasn't far away — when my feet began to ache too much I could veer into the water anytime I wanted and instantly find refreshment. The Gulf was always there to wash away my pain and give me a fresh new start along my path, no matter where I had walked or how much trouble my feet got into.

As I looked out at the Gulf, this wonderful source of comfort, I was awed that it would even have anything to do with me — it was much too important and much too busy to be concerned with the likes of me. The Gulf seemed infinite — as far as I looked I could not see the end of it. As enormous as it was I knew it had many responsibilities and too many things to do. It had too many other creatures depending on it to be concerned with my little feet.

This Gulf provided coastline for five American states, as well as eastern Mexico and the entire island of Cuba. It had to provide life for the many creatures who live in it: red snapper, flounder, shrimp, mullet, oysters, crabs, tarpon, mackerel, porpoises, dolphins and many others who depend upon the Gulf for life.

The Gulf has to provide a livelihood for the fishermen who work there. It must provide recreation for the people who come to it for swimming, sailing and water-skiing. It must support the many ships that sail upon it. The warm Gulf Stream air it circulates helps to lessen the effects of winter in parts of western Europe.

In short, the Gulf was an immensely powerful being, seemingly infinite with millions of people and animals depending upon it for life. Yet with everything else it had to do, this enormous Gulf was still able to reach out its water to my little size 8 $1/2$ feet and give them comfort. With all its other responsibilities, it seemed to know about me and to care about me!

As I thought about this I realized that God must work in the same way. He too is an immense being with millions of people, animals and plants to care for and have a relationship with. But there is always a part of him available to us, no matter how small or insignificant we feel. Like the Gulf of Mexico he is able to include *everyone* who comes to him, no matter *how many* come. There's plenty of him to go around.

As I further thought about the Gulf I realized that this water, just like God, was not there just for the painful times. That water was always going to be there for as long as I journeyed along the beach. Even when the sand was pleasant to walk in the Gulf was still there, inviting me to enjoy its waters *anytime*, to splash and play in them. As long as I journey in my life God will always be there too, in good times as well as bad. He invites me to come to him *anytime*, to simply enjoy being with him and to love him. No matter how big or powerful he seems, he always has a place for me.

King David must have felt the same way when he wrote Psalm 8. It goes like this:

When I look up into the night skies and see the work of your fingers — the moon and the stars you have made — I cannot understand how you can bother with mere puny man, to pay any attention to him! And yet you have made him only a little lower than the angels and placed a crown of glory and honor upon his head. You have put him in charge of everything you made; everything is put under his authority: all sheep and oxen, and wild animals too, the birds and fish, and all the life in the sea. O Jehovah, our Lord, the majesty and glory of you have filled the earth.

Psalm 8:3-9

If God forgives us anyway, what difference does it make if we sin?

Now that we've talked about how loving and forgiving God is, this is an important question to consider.

This question, in fact, puzzled me for years. I was always taught that sin was a terrible thing, and that God did not want us to sin. But I was also taught that God always forgives sin if we're really sorry, and gives us a new start. It would thus seem to follow that it makes no difference if we sin. If God forgives us, everything's okay, right?

Wrong. Even with God's forgiveness, sin makes a *big* difference in our lives. Sin leads to some serious consequences which even God's forgiveness can't reverse.

Suppose you are having an argument with a friend. In your anger you grab a baseball sitting on the table and throw it through a window. You later apologize to your friend, and you are forgiven. Does that mean that your fit of anger made no difference? Of course not!

First of all, there is still a broken window that needs to be repaired — forgiveness didn't change that. Second, even though your friend has forgiven you, you hurt him a lot which will probably change the way he acts toward you in the future. Having seen your temper he'll be more careful around you, less open, less trusting, more suspicious. He might even like you a little less, and may question how good a friend you really are.

Your tantrum will also affect your relationships with other people. Your friend's parents will no longer trust you around their house, and will be anxious about having you around. Your parents will be upset by your actions, and may restrict how often you can go out. When your friends hear about what you did (and they will, because people love to gossip), it will change the way they think about you and act towards you. Some might make fun of you, hurting your feelings. If younger kids saw or heard about you throwing the baseball they may imitate your actions in times of anger, and this whole scene will be repeated over and over.

There is no such thing as a sin without consequences. Anything we do which hurts ourselves or others spreads like a germ, infecting people in ways we can't even see. It certainly does make a difference if we sin, even when God forgives us. The results of our actions can last long after we have been forgiven.

An excellent commentary on this is given in *The Way Bible*. It goes like this:

> Forgiveness cannot erase all consequences. We celebrate the love and forgiveness of God, and rightly so. His mercy is everlasting. His love goes on forever.
> A simple, honest expression of faith throws open the doors of God's heaven and rolls out a welcome mat for us. God tosses out a blanket of forgiveness to fully cover our sins. He gives us a new beginning, a brand new start.
> God's forgiveness is so complete we might think it leaves nothing uncovered, nothing unresolved. When God forgives, what could possibly remain of sin?

The consequences. The embarrassing
   results. The chain of events sin sets in
   motion.

That's why we should try our best to avoid
sin, despite the promise of forgiveness. Avoiding
sin just makes the world a better place; stumbling
into sin only worsens things.

When it comes down to it, trying to live a
good, moral Christian life is just common sense.
When we try to live the ideals of love and forgiveness, when we work to help suffering people ease
their pain, when we let go of our anger and try to
live in peace with one another, we're a lot happier.
We're not perfectly happy, because we're imperfect and we make mistakes. But true happiness is
found only in *goodness*. That's a fact nobody can
deny.

The misery we experience occurs when people
choose not to seek goodness. When we stay angry
with people, mock people who are different from
us, when we ignore people's pain, when we hurt
others to help ourselves, when we glorify what is
ugly — violence, death, destruction — instead of
what is beautiful — peace, eternal life, creation —
then we're unhappy. The search for truth and
goodness leads to happiness. The search for what
is false and bad leads to unhappiness. When you
look at it, it's really just common sense.

That's why we try not to sin, because even with God's forgiveness, sin makes the world a tougher place in which to live.

Is there really a hell, and why would God send people there if he loves them?

Yes, there really is a hell. The Bible speaks plainly about it many times. Yes, God loves the people in hell, for God's love is so perfect it extends to everyone. But God does not send people to hell; people go there of their own choosing by freely deciding to reject God and his offer of eternal life with him.

Nobody knows for sure what hell is like — just as nobody knows for sure what heaven is like. We usually picture hell as a place of terrible torture, with flames of fire creating unbearable heat and suffering. Jesus himself speaks of hell as a place of fire. But instead of being caught up in that kind of imagery, what we really need to know about hell is what it *basically* is: being separated from God forever. Whatever other experiences might be in store in hell, the worst possible destiny for anyone is to spend all of eternity away from God, because that means being away from the *experience* of his love. Living forever without the most incredible, perfect love imaginable has got to result in nothing but misery. That's basically what hell is — living apart from the loving presence of God. Jesus' talk about fire emphasizes what a miserable experience hell must be.

Jesus promises heaven to *all* who believe in him and live for him, and *all* who trust in him to take away the consequences of their sins. Read carefully these words of his:

> How earnestly I tell you this — anyone who believes in me already has eternal life! *John 6:47*

Notice how Jesus didn't say that those who trust him *will* have eternal life, or *might* have eternal life. He said they *already* have it! Living our lives for Jesus and trusting in him to take away our punishment through God's mercy *automatically* gets us to heaven! We don't have to be worried or anxious about it. Heaven is not some exclusive club where you have to meet a strict set of requirements and only a few get in. It's open to *everyone* who chooses to love God and follow Jesus in their life, no matter how many mistakes they make:

> For God loved the world so much that he gave his only Son so that anyone who believes in him shall not perish but

have eternal life. God did not send his Son into the world to condemn it, but to save it. There is no eternal doom awaiting those who trust him to save them. But those who don't trust him have already been tried and condemned.

John 3:16-18

If we truly believe in Jesus, genuinely repent of our sins and sincerely ask God's forgiveness, we will go to heaven. Hell is reserved only for those people who have freely chosen to reject God and the life he offers and have chosen instead to live for themselves or for something other than God. There is no sin, no matter how serious, that cannot be forgiven and heaven gained if a person truly desires to return to God and puts his trust in his Son Jesus. Anyone who sincerely longs for God and shows this through his actions will come to be with God in heaven. It is only when someone gives up on God and the promise of eternal life in his wonderful love that he chooses hell for himself.

What is purgatory?

We've learned that God does not "send" people to hell. The only people who end up in hell are those who have freely chosen to be there. If we have lived our lives for God and truly want to be with him (and have proven this desire not just with *words*, but by our *actions*), he will take us to heaven to be with him, no matter what we have done. Our life on earth is actually a *process* of moving away from our human imperfection and moving towards the perfection of God:

> You are to be perfect, even as your Father in heaven is perfect.
>
> *Matthew 5:48*

We don't do it all at once, nor do we accomplish most of it when we are young. It's a *life-long* process with many steps and stages.

Purgatory is the final stage in reaching the perfection which God ultimately intends for us. Before I explain what it is, I'd like to use the following example to help illustrate how we use our lives to become more like the people God made us to be.

Imagine you're going swimming in a lake. As you stand on the beach ready to go, you can't just dive right in because the water is too shallow — you're not yet ready to swim. So you walk into the water and it's only about as high as your ankles. You're not ready yet. So you walk further until the water is up to your knees. You're still not ready.

You walk still further until the water reaches your thighs and then your hips, but you're still not ready for a good swim. So you walk even further until your body is far enough under water that you can "take the plunge" and finally enjoy your swim. It's the reward for the effort you made to journey that far out into the water.

Now just like our example with the Gulf of Mexico, think of that lake water as God. Your goal in life is to "take the plunge" into him and become completely immersed in him and covered with his refreshing love. But reaching that point of total immersion in God comes only after a long journey in which you are *little by little* drawn into him.

At this point in your life, as you're just beginning a real mature relationship with God, you're just ankle-deep in that shallow end. As the years go by, if you really want to go on that swim with him, you'll get a little deeper and deeper. As an adult you won't be to that deep part yet, but you'll be much further than you are now. Just how far you'll go will depend on your desire and your commitment to really know God and live his kind of life.

Plunging in for that swim is heaven — when you are finally, *completely* in God and he in you. But we have to journey through all of the stages to get there. Most of us end our earthly lives still in the shallower areas. We did not try hard enough or move fast enough through those shallow parts to reach a deep relationship with God while on earth, and our time runs out before we can get ready to dive in. Purgatory is the time between death and heaven where God helps us to get through the rest of those waters and come to a *perfect* knowledge of him. Only then are we ready to enter his eternal kingdom.

Some people think of purgatory as a place of punishment, that it's a place for people who love God but sinned too much so they must be punished before entering heaven. But remember that Jesus took away *all* punishment for sin. Purgatory is a place to *continue* and *complete* our life-long journey to God, so that we can enter his kingdom completely free of our human imperfection.

Purgatory is a time of purification, of growing, of improving. Like any growing that we do in our lives, it necessarily involves some pain and discomfort. But once we've finished that final stage of transformation we'll reach our goal of perfection, and be with God and his incredible love forever.

Why does it seem like a lot of people who go to church are hypocrites?

One of the main reasons many people give for not going to church goes something like this: "The people there are nothing but hypocrites. They go to church on Sunday, but during the rest of the week they're sinners." The answer to this is simple: That's exactly *why* people go to church on Sunday — because they *are* sinners!

Some people have the idea that church is a restricted area where only the pure and holy belong. They think that church is some sort of privilege only for those who live perfect lives, and anyone who's in the habit of sinning has no business being there.

But the reason we go to church is because we're *not* holy — we *are* sinners and we need God's help to put our lives on the right path. If we weren't sinners we'd have no need to go to church — we'd be as perfect as God, and we wouldn't need him at all. But we do need him, and that's the reason we go to church — not to "show off" to people how wonderful we are, but to acknowledge our weakness, imperfection and sinfulness, and to ask for help from God and from our fellow believers.

Jesus made it very clear that he came to earth for a certain type of person:

That night Levi invited his fellow tax collectors and many other notorious sinners to be his dinner guests so that they could meet Jesus and his disciples. (There were many men of this type among the crowds that followed him.) But when some of the Jewish religious leaders saw him eating with these men of ill repute, they said to his disciples, "How can he stand it, to eat with such scum?" When Jesus heard what they were saying, he told them, "Sick people need the doctor, not healthy ones! I haven't come to tell good people to repent, but the bad ones."

Mark 2:15-17

Jesus not only realized it was sinners who needed him the most, but he had tremendous compassion and love for sinners, not a judgmental attitude. He looked at sinners as candidates for heaven, not as garbage to be thrown away. He saw in them opportunities to spread God's love and plant it in their hearts, not opportunities to be snobbish and condemning. Jesus' love for sinners is so intense it led him to perform the greatest act of love the world has ever known — freely giving his life on the cross so that sinners may return to God.

Jesus freely chose to undergo the crucifixion.

He could have backed out, but his love was too perfect. He put the needs of God's people ahead of his own convenience, and freely underwent an inhuman, grueling torture out of love for people who disobey God's will. It's the same kind of love he calls us to have for sinners, a love that is compassionate and recognizes their need to have God in their lives.

So if some people in church seem like hypocrites, remember the reason they're really there — to admit their sinfulness and to ask God and their fellow believers for love and support. Then do whatever you can to give them that love and support.

Why do I have to go to church? Can't I just believe in Jesus — isn't that enough?

Many people don't see a need for organized religion. They see church as an inadequate and unnecessary organization, full of bumbling human beings who make too many mistakes to be really effective in bringing people to God. Many people feel they can be a more effective Christian by worshiping God "privately." They can go to him whenever they want without having to depend on services organized by others. As long as they're living good Christian lives they see no need to join a church. They feel they belong to God as much as anyone in a church, so it should make no difference whether or not they attend.

This sounds convincing, but it leaves out some important details. Namely, that God created people to live in *faith communities* where they would *share* God with each other to help strengthen each other. We come to God through love of neighbor, so we need neighbors to love. It simply can't be done "privately."

St. Paul explains this dependence upon one another in his first letter to the Corinthians. He compares the church to the human body; it is made up of many parts, none of which can function separately from the rest of the members:

> Our bodies have many parts, but the many parts make up only one body when they are all put together. So it is with the "body" of Christ. Each of us is a part of the one body of Christ. . . . Yes, the body has many parts, not just one part. . . . Suppose the whole body were an eye — then how would you hear? Or if your whole body were just one big ear, how could you smell anything? But that isn't the way God has made us. He has made many parts of our bodies and

has put each part just where he wants it. What a strange thing a body would be if it had only one part! So he has made many parts, but still there is only one body. The eye can never say to the hand, "I don't need you." The head can't say to the feet, "I don't need you."
1 Corinthians 12:12-14, 17-21

Paul further writes in his letter to the Ephesians about the need for *communities* to bring together the talents of many so that all may benefit, so that these many parts may truly become one body:

Why is it that he gives us these special abilities to do certain things best? It is that God's people will be equipped to do better work for him, building up the church, the body of Christ, to a position of strength and maturity; until finally we all believe alike about our salvation and about our Savior, God's Son, and all become full grown in the Lord — yes, to the point of being filled full with Christ. Then we will no longer be like children, forever changing our minds about what we believe because someone has told us something different or has cleverly lied to us and made the lie sound like the truth. Instead, we will lovingly follow the truth at all times — speaking truly, living truly — and so become more and more in every way like Christ, who is the Head of his body, the church. Under his direction, the whole body is fitted together perfectly, and each part in its own special way helps the other parts, so that the whole body is healthy and growing and full of love.   *Ephesians 4:12-16*

Our faith life is never a "private" affair. By its very nature, our life in God is designed to be inter-active with people, to use the gifts he's given us to bring him to others and strengthen his "body," the church. As St. Paul says, *all* the members are needed. Parts cannot live apart from the body, and the body can't live without its parts.

God blesses us through the community of believers. We have to gather in community to be part of his body. There may be many things we don't like about going to church. It may seem boring; there may be other things we'd rather do; we may not like some of the people who are there; it may seem like a waste of time. But if we really believe in God, if we truly long for life with him, we need to gather in faith communities and pray for one another.

Church becomes meaningful in our lives if

we understand why we're there, and if we participate *in our hearts* and not just with words. It may not always seem like something important is happening, but if our hearts are really tuned to God he'll be with us, whether we can *sense* his presence or not.

What specifically does the church do for me?

We can't see or hear God the Father, the Son, or the Holy Spirit. Remember, God made us less than himself. We're not powerful enough as human beings to be able to find God with our limited senses. We need to experience God through each other in the community of the church. To do this, Jesus gave the church seven special actions called sacraments, through which people have a special encounter with God and receive a special blessing from him through his church. Since we need God to live and we need the church to know God, these sacraments are powerful times which bring God, the church and people together. As such they're the most powerful gifts we can receive from God on earth.

Lets take a quick look at each of the seven sacraments and see what they do for us.

Baptism

When we're born, we begin a life which will one day come to an end. Every person born into the world will eventually leave the world; everyone dies at some point. The life we are born into is temporary, destined to end in death.

But God wants all people to be born into *his* life, the one which never ends. Though the body stops working at some point, the soul lives forever. It can return to God in total happiness (eventually to be clothed with a glorified body) if it is born into the life of God. Baptism is our "re-birth" into this life with God. The waters of baptism wash away the power our sins have over us to keep us apart from God, and give us the eternal life of Christ. In baptism we "die to death" so that Jesus can raise us to new life. It is the first step in living the Christian life.

Reconciliation

We all sin. We all do things that go against God's ways. To continue living in the way that will lead us to eternal life, we need to ask for God's forgiveness. He never refuses! God forgives everyone who is truly sorry for their sins, and never grows tired of giving people new chances.

The sacrament of reconciliation is a *celebra-*

tion of God's forgiveness. We come to church, confess our sins to a priest, receive the forgiveness of God and leave in the joy of his love.

Yet many people believe this sacrament is unnecessary. They say they can confess to God privately in prayer and ask for forgiveness, and he will give it. They don't see the need for going to a priest to receive God's forgiveness when they can receive the same forgiveness through private prayer.

It's true that God forgives us just by being sorry and by simply telling him. Lots of forgiveness takes place outside the reconciliation room. But when we sin, no matter what kind of sin it is, we sin against more than God. All sin weakens the church, Christ's body on earth. When the church forgives us in the name of Christ who gave the church special power to do so, we *know* we are forgiven. And the priest's forgiveness brings us a sense of peace and reassurance that nothing else can. We need the priest, the representative of the church, to forgive us on behalf of the whole church family.

Remember the example of throwing the baseball through the window? Even when God forgives, there are still consequences to live with. To fully make up for our sins, we also need to make up with the people we've offended, to restore the human relationship that was damaged. In the sacrament of reconciliation, the priest forgives us on behalf of the whole church, so we can once again resume our place as a strong member of the body of Christ. Rather than a thing to be feared and avoided, it is an event to be celebrated.

Holy Communion

In this sacrament, Jesus makes himself present to us in the form of bread and wine. Jesus promised us that when we join ourselves to his death and resurrection we too will gain eternal life. We must then share in the broken body and spilled blood of Jesus if we are to rise with him. Jesus makes his sacrificed body and blood available to us in Holy Communion. Through the actions of the priest, Jesus actually makes the bread and wine his body and blood. By sharing in it we share in his death and thus his resurrection as well. This is why Jesus says he is the "Bread of Life."

Confirmation

In this sacrament, we receive the fullness of the Holy Spirit, and make a formal commitment to live our lives for Jesus in the community of the church. Confirmation increases and deepens the gifts we received at baptism. It unites us more strongly with the Father, Son and Holy Spirit, strengthens our bond with the church, and gives us the special help of the Holy Spirit.

Marriage

In this sacrament a man and a woman accept each other as God's gifts to one another, and make a commitment to love each other the way God loves his people. They acknowledge that their marriage is not something they are doing by themselves, not something to be taken lightly. Rather, like all other sacraments, it is an action of God in which he makes himself present through the church. God has involved himself in the life of the couple through marriage. They promise to honor their commitment to love each other till death as their way of living out their lives for God.

Holy Orders

In this sacrament, a man responds to an invitation from God and from the church to dedicate his life solely to the service of God's people as a priest. Through this sacrament God not only involves himself in the life of the priest, but through him God touches all the people he will minister to. The priest becomes an instrument through which God's love can reach his people. Since the priest is the one who gives sacraments to the people, this sacrament actually helps give life to the others.

Anointing of the Sick

In this sacrament, the church gives a special blessing to those who are very ill. Jesus has tremendous compassion for everyone who suffers physical ailments. In this sacrament the sick are blessed with a special oil to give them the comfort of Christ as they struggle to endure their suffering. Through this sacrament the person's sins are forgiven, so they don't have to worry about being reconciled to God while they deal with their illness. Frequently they feel better physically and occasionally they are even healed.

These seven sacraments are God's ways of working through his church to touch the lives of his people. As persons yearning for God, we should try to participate in the sacraments as often as we can.

So how do I get to know God?

The story I told earlier about the Gulf of Mexico is one example of how we get to know God — by looking for his likeness in the things he created. God was actually speaking to me that day through the symbol of the water — I was just attentive enough to listen to him.

Reading helps us to know him. This is especially so in the case of the Bible, which is the inspired word of God and should be read prayerfully. We get to know God also through our relationships with other people, for when people accept God in their lives he works through them and they share him with us. But the best way to really form a relationship with God and to get to know him is through prayer.

Prayer is one of the hardest things you'll ever have to do if you want a real relationship with God. When we're little kids we learn to "say our prayers," which involves either reciting memorized words or saying something to God, usually thanking him or asking him for something. But to have a mature relationship with God you must learn to do more than talk to him. You must learn to *listen* to him and to just *be* with him.

Think of a good friend that you have. Would you ever go to their house, recite some memorized words, then leave without giving them a chance to respond? Would you talk to your friend only when you wanted to ask for something? Would you ever have any kind of conversation with your friends where you did all of the talking and didn't give them a chance to speak?

Of course not, because a friendship like that wouldn't last very long. Real friends both talk *and* listen to each other, because that's the only way to really get to know someone. When people become really good friends there are times when they don't even have to talk to each other at all — they just enjoy being in each other's company, and no conversation is necessary.

This is the kind of friendship God wants with us. He wants us to talk to him, he wants us to *listen* to him, and he wants us to enjoy just being with him without any conversation at all. Real prayer involves all three.

Most of us have the talking part down pretty good — as human beings we generally talk better than we listen! But how do we listen to God while we're praying? How can we just sit there and be with him without any speaking going on? And how do we know if praying really works?

Let me answer each of these questions one at a time.

First of all, to do any kind of praying, we need to take some time out of our day and make that time specifically for prayer. Ten minutes a day is a good way to start. See if you can set aside ten minutes of your day to go to a quiet place by yourself and spend that time with God. Try to put everything else out of your mind and focus on being with God. If your heart really desires to be with him, he'll be there — even if it doesn't seem like he's there. (One of the hardest things about prayer is that a lot of the time it seems like nothing's happening, that God's not really there and it's a waste of time. I'll talk about that in a bit.)

Talking to God comes easy. But how do we listen to him? There are a lot of ways. Sometimes God speaks to us in our imaginations. He puts thoughts into our minds, thoughts that seem to come from nowhere, as his way of giving us ideas. Sometimes he speaks to us in our hearts, giving us the desire to do something he wants us to do. Sometimes he speaks to us through events that occur after we pray; something happens in our life and we just know it came from God. Sometimes he speaks to us through symbols — my experience at the Gulf of Mexico was actually God speaking to me through the symbolism of the water. I was just attentive enough to listen. Sometimes he speaks to us through our reading of the Bible. A lot of times it helps to read a passage from the Bible before praying, then think about what we read in the presence of God. (At the end of this book I've included a list of Bible quotes that are good "prayer starters.")

When we really turn our hearts to God and focus on him as the center of our lives, we begin to hear him speaking to us in all kinds of ways — some obvious, some very subtle. It's similar to a radio. The air is full of radio waves we can't see with our eyes or hear with our ears. They are constantly being sent out to give us information and enjoyment, but we can't hear them until we turn on a radio and tune it to a particular frequency. God's messages are like those radio waves, and our hearts are the radios. God is constantly speaking to us, but we can't hear him with our ears. Only when we turn on our hearts and tune them to God's frequency will we hear what he has to say. Sometimes it takes a lot of tuning to find his "station," but if we're persistent we'll eventually find him.

Sometimes God doesn't say anything to us at all in prayer. Like a good friend, he just wants to be with us without having to talk at all. When our prayer time is like that, when neither God nor us are saying anything, it gets pretty boring and frustrating. It feels like a waste of time — like we're just sitting there and nothing is happening. It seems like God isn't even there.

This gets pretty discouraging, because when we pray we want to get "good feelings." We want to feel a sense of peace, of truly "being in touch" with God, being filled with joy and love and fired up to go out and be his disciples. But more often than not when we pray things feel very ordinary, and it is very easy to think that we're wasting time because nothing is happening.

St. Teresa of Avila explained that kind of "boring" prayer very well, using the example of a garden. She said that in each of us God has planted a garden of "virtues," or good qualities. We are the gardeners, responsible for making sure that these virtues grow. In order to grow they need water, and that's what prayer is. The gardener's job is to get water for the *flowers* — not for himself. Water is to make the flowers grow, it is not for the gardener's own enjoyment. The true measure of the gardener's success is not how good he feels while watering, but how well his flowers are growing.

Our prayer, like the gardener's water, is not for our own enjoyment. It is so that our virtues may grow. When we're in prayer and we're not feeling anything special, it is because the water of our prayer is going to the garden of our virtues and not to satisfy our own thirst. The most effective prayer results not in all kinds of wonderful feelings, but in our virtues growing and we becoming better people as a result. So when we pray and nothing happens, we have to trust that God is working in us, even though we can't feel it, to make us better people.

Author Thomas J. Green uses an excellent modern day example to explain what that kind of prayer is like. He compares it to surgery. God is the surgeon, we are the patient, and the operation is prayer. Just as the patient is put to sleep while the surgeon works, we can't see or feel God working on us as we pray. Just like the patient, many times we don't feel much better right after God has worked on us. But as time goes on the improvements God made will show themselves in our lives, even though we couldn't actually feel him do it at the time. We're so used to getting what we want right away, but God's work takes longer than the world's ways, and we have to learn to wait patiently for him.

We also have to realize that God works in us throughout our whole lives. He made us imperfect copies of himself, in the hopes that we would choose to become more like him. For those who make this choice, it is a *life-long* process of becoming perfect very *slowly* and in seemingly small steps. In some people God seems to work slower than in others. But he's always working. We have to trust him to work at his own pace.

Part Three:
THIS ALL SOUNDS GOOD, BUT...

As I've said already, living a Christian life is really just common sense. Since God designed the world, things can only work well when his guidelines are followed.

Naturally we're happier when we love and accept each other without prejudice, resentment or suspicion, when we forgive each other, believe in each other, and refuse to give up on each other. Living these ideas only improves the world and our lives in it. It's just common sense.

Naturally we're more secure and confident when we can trust a greater, more powerful being than ourselves to be the guiding force in our lives, to take away our guilt and lead us to a life that never ends. This kind of trust only improves the world and our lives in it. It's just common sense.

Naturally we're more at peace when we stop complaining about the problems in the world and accept them as a result of its imperfection, resolving to do whatever we can to make things better instead of adding to the problems. This only improves the world and our lives in it. It's just common sense.

The light of God's wisdom and love improves the world with the promise of hope. The darkness of being without God destroys the world with the doom of despair. It's just that simple. But it's so hard to live by! We're always meeting people who don't live according to God's designs, and the pressure they can put on us makes our work of spreading his light to them that much harder. Jesus realized how many people reject God's ways when he said:

> The Light from heaven came into the world, but they loved the darkness more than the light, for their deeds were evil. They hated the heavenly light because they wanted to sin in the darkness.
> *John 3:19-20*

Some people laugh at us for trying to live according to God's light, and pressure us to join them in the ways of darkness. They see the pleasures the world has to offer — money and all the things it can buy, alcohol, sex, drugs — and can't understand why anyone wouldn't put these pleasures at the center of their life. They see Christians as people who simply don't like to have fun, and a lot of times they make fun of us for being so "straight-laced" or "goody-goody."

It's true that the world has a lot of pleasures that are very attractive and more visible than the kind of rewards God offers. But let's take a very careful look at what happens to us as people when we look to those pleasures as goals in our life, to find out *why* Christians look elsewhere to find fulfillment.

At the very root of the world's pleasures, what really makes them attractive, is that they satisfy *our* desires. That may not seem like such a bad thing, but think about what that does to a person over time. The more we make a habit of satisfying our own desires — be it for money, possessions, sex, or whatever — the more self-centered we become. When we make a habit of putting *our* wants first and make them the driving force in our life, we make ourselves less appealing to other people — they see us as being selfish and won't want to have anything to do with us. When we turn inwards looking for happiness instead of outwards, this naturally leads to loneliness and sadness. Many people who think that Christians try to take the "fun" out of life learn that the kind of "fun" they enjoy usually leads only to problems.

Rather than searching after pleasures that will satisfy *our* wants, if instead we can make ourselves sensitive to the needs of *others*, and serve them the way God teaches us, we bring more love to the world. As a result, *we're* loved more, and we become happier. We turn ourselves outward, find love from others, and become *really* happy. Because when it comes down to it, *love* is what really brings us joy in life. True Christian love among people actually brings more joy into the world through lasting, supportive relationships, and makes the world a happier place. It's just common sense.

Being loved and cared for by another person and returning that love and care is a greater feeling than any amount of money, drink, casual sex, or anything else the world holds before us as goals.

Our life on earth is very short compared to the eternal life God promises to all who live for him. If our lives are spent not centered on him but on the goods and pleasures of this passing earth, not only will our lives be less rewarding here but our lives in the next world will be empty as well:

> Anyone who keeps his life for himself shall lose it; and anyone who loses his life for me shall find it again. What profit is there if you gain the whole world — and lose eternal life? What can

be compared with the value of eternal
life?   *Matthew 16:25-26*

The temptations of the world are strong. So
are the pressures people put on us to give in to
those temptations. But God's strength is stronger,
and is able to overcome any pressure mere human
beings are able to put on us.

Jesus was mocked, criticized, laughed at,
persecuted and killed by people who thought his
way of life was weird. He overcame all of that —for
us — conquering the death the world put him to
and rising to the glorious everlasting life of God.

It is that same strength of Jesus, not our own
feeble strength, that we can call upon in times
when we're made fun of or pressured to do things
we know go against God's wishes:

> I've told you these things so you'll have
> peace in me; you'll have suffering in the
> world, but take courage! I've conquered
> the world!   *John 16:33*

I said at the start of this book that I can't give
you the answers to all of your questions about God,
but I can give you *some*. My intent has been to teach
you enough about God so you could put aside any
other notions you may have had about him and
begin to know him as he really is. It takes a lifetime

to really learn about God, but I can promise you that you'll have a wonderful life if you put him at the center and keep him as your goal. Your life won't be perfect — you'll still have plenty of problems and setbacks. But you'll have a powerful friend to help you along and to welcome you home to heaven some day, no matter how many times you've failed along the way.

This book was a start — so where do you go from here? For one thing, you can do more reading. The Bible is a great place to start. At the end of this book I've made a list of some of my favorite Bible passages, the ones that have meant the most to me in my journey so far of getting to know God. I hope you'll take some time to look them up and read them yourself, and that you'll also find them a source of inspiration and wisdom.

Another thing to do is to share your faith with others — remember, your faith life is not a private affair. If you know an adult who has an active faith life and whom you trust, talk to him or her. They can give you good advice on how to live your faith in the specific situations of your life. Check with your church to see if they have any programs for people your age. A lot of parishes have youth groups which give young people a chance to share their faith and strengthen it in a supportive community.

Most importantly, pray often. Re-read my

section on "So how do I get to know God?" if you're not sure where to begin or what to expect.

There is no greater feeling than knowing you were made by the same being who created the entire universe, that he crafted you with the same care and loves you with the same love. You're just as important as the most imposing mountain, deepest ocean or beautiful rainbow — in fact, even more so:

> Look at the birds! They don't worry about what to eat — they don't need to sow or reap or store up food — your heavenly Father feeds them. And you are far more valuable to him than they are. . . . And if God cares so wonderfully for flowers that are here today and gone tomorrow, won't he more surely care for you, O men of little faith?
>
> *Matthew 6:26, 30*

There is no greater experience than having a real relationship with that incredible being who made the whole world, making him an active part of your world and the center of your life. Invite him into your heart, and I hope you will be able to join me in my prayer:

"When you in your infinite genius, O God, created the earth, the sun, the moon, the stars, the seas, the mountains, the rivers, valleys, birds, animals, rainbows, winds, clouds, flowers and trees — thanks for also thinking of me!"

James Penrice
Grand Rapids, Michigan
August 28, Feast of St. Augustine
(One of the biggest sinners
ever to become a saint!)

List of
SUGGESTED BIBLE READINGS

This is a list of my favorite passages from the Bible (in addition to the ones I already used in the book). If you're looking for a way to begin praying, I suggest reading one of these passages and then quietly praying over it for ten minutes. With the combination of God's word and his presence in prayer, I'm confident that it will prove a good experience for you, and give you a good start in your mature relationship with God. I hope you will eventually use all of them, then will explore the Bible yourself and discover the many riches it has to offer.

Key: Jeremiah 17:7-8 means the book of Jeremiah, chapter 17, verses 7 through 8.

Psalm 139
Isaiah 55
Jeremiah 17:7-8

Jeremiah 18:1-6
Matthew 5:1-12
Matthew 6:19-34
Matthew 11:27-30
Matthew 19:25-30
Luke 15:11-32
John 6:35-40
Romans 5:8-10
Romans 8:38-39
Romans 10:8-10
Romans 12:2
1 Corinthians 1:26-29
1 Corinthians 10:13
1 Corinthians 13:1-3
2 Corinthians 4:16-18
Galatians 2:20
Galatians 5:22-24
Ephesians 3:8-9
Philippians 4:6-7
Colossians 2:6-10
1 Timothy 1:15-17
2 Timothy 3:1-5
Titus 2:11-15
Hebrews 13:8-9
James 1:5-8
James 2:17
1 John 2:15-17
1 John 5:21

BIBLIOGRAPHY

All Scripture verses (except John 16:33) are taken
from *The Living Bible*, copyright 1971. Used
by permission of Tyndale House Publishers,
Inc., Wheaton, IL 60189. All rights reserved.

John 16:33 is taken from *The Alba House Gospels:
So You May Believe*. Mark A. Wauck, trans.
Alba House, 1992.

"Only the Good Die Young" is from *The Stranger*
by Billy Joel, copyright 1977, CBS, Inc.,
51 W. 52nd Street, New York, NY.

The discussions of St. Teresa of Avila and Thomas
Green are based on passages from *When the
Well Runs Dry* by Thomas H. Green, SJ.
Copyright 1979 by Ave Maria Press, Notre
Dame, IN 46556.

The discussion of love as a commitment instead of
a feeling is based on a passage from *Unconditional Love* by John Powell, SJ. Copyright
1978, Tabor Publishing, Allen, TX.

This book was designed and published by St. Pauls/Alba House, the publishing arm of the Society of St. Paul, an international religious congregation of priests and brothers dedicated to serving the Church through the communications media. For information regarding this and associated ministries of the Pauline Family of Congregations, write to the Vocation Director, Society of St. Paul, 7050 Pinehurst, Dearborn, Michigan 48126 or check our internet site, www.albahouse.org